Making a Global Impact

Lorin Driggs

Reader Consultants

Brian Allman, M.A.
Classroom Teacher, West Virginia

Cheryl Norman Lane, M.A.Ed.
Classroom Teacher
Chino Valley Unified School District

iCivics Consultants

Emma Humphries, Ph.D.
Chief Education Officer

Taylor Davis, M.T.
Director of Curriculum and Content

Natacha Scott, MAT
Director of Educator Engagement

Publishing Credits

Rachelle Cracchiolo, M.S.Ed., *Publisher*
Emily R. Smith, M.A.Ed., *VP of Content Development*
Véronique Bos, *Creative Director*
Dona Herweck Rice, *Senior Content Manager*
Dani Neiley, *Associate Editor*
Fabiola Sepulveda, *Series Designer*
Cynthia Paul, *Illustrator pages 6–9*

Image Credits: p4 Shutterstock/nutcd32; p10 FDR Presidential Library & Museum; p11 top Shutterstock/Sean Pavone; p11 bottom Shutterstock/Dietmar Temps; p12 botom Shutterstock/Djohan Shahrin; p13 Getty Images/Louisa Gouliamaki; p14 Newscom/ Ton Koene/VWPics; p15 Getty Images/AFP/Stringer; p19 Alamy/ Reuters; p20 Alamy/Guy Oliver; p21 Shutterstock/Robert Podlaski; p22 Shutterstock/ Jonathan Weiss; p23 top Alamy/Tribune Content Agency LLC; p23 bottom Torbjorn Toby Jorgensen; p25 Getty Images/Nigel Waldron; p26 Newscom/Kevin Lamarque/REUTERS; p27 top Getty Images/Gallo Images; p27 bottom Beautiful News SA; p28 Shutterstock/ Simone Hogan; p29 Getty Images/Rick Diamond; all other photos by iStock and/or Shutterstock

Library of Congress Cataloging-in-Publication Data

Names: Driggs, Lorin, author. | iCivics (Organization)
Title: Making a global impact / Lorin Driggs.
Description: Huntington Beach, CA : Teacher Created Materials, 2022. | "iCivics"--Cover. | Audience: Grades 4-6 | Summary: "Human rights are universal. But they are not always universally available. Poverty, war, disease, and other challenges prevent some people around the world from having their basic human rights. Many organizations and people are dedicated to helping them"-- Provided by publisher.
Identifiers: LCCN 2021054846 (print) | LCCN 2021054847 (ebook) | ISBN 9781087615516 (paperback) | ISBN 9781087630625 (ebook)
Subjects: LCSH: Human rights--Juvenile literature.
Classification: LCC JC571 .D83 2022 (print) | LCC JC571 (ebook) | DDC 323--dc23/eng/20211203
LC record available at https://lccn.loc.gov/2021054846
LC ebook record available at https://lccn.loc.gov/2021054847

TCM Teacher Created Materials
5482 Argosy Avenue
Huntington Beach, CA 92649
www.tcmpub.com

ISBN 978-1-0876-1551-6

Table of Contents

The Human Rights Challenge

A serious disease breaks out in a country. Medical care is not available. Elsewhere, after a long **drought**, a small farm cannot support the family that owns it. And in still another country, the government wants to let a mining company take over land without consulting the people who live there. In many parts of the world, plastic pollutes the land and seas. It puts humans and wildlife in danger. In some places, racial **discrimination** continues, even when it is against the law.

What do all these events have in common? They are about human rights. All humans have certain rights the moment they are born. But human rights are not always respected and protected. Fortunately, there are organizations and people who care. They take action when human rights are denied. They find solutions. Many of them make a global impact by helping other people.

Jump into Fiction

Maya's Bright Idea
A HOME IN SAN ANTONIO, TEXAS
THE SUPER FALCONS WIN AGAIN! I KNEW THEY WOULD!
REALLY? HOW COULD YOU KNOW?
THEY COULDN'T LOSE. THEY'RE THE BEST TEAM IN THE WHOLE STATE!
LOOK. THE TEAM CAPTAIN IS SPEAKING.
WE WANT TO SHARE OUR GOOD FORTUNE WITH OTHERS. WE DEDICATE THIS WIN TO THE WATER PROJECT. WE URGE ALL OUR FANS TO CONTRIBUTE TO THEIR IMPORTANT WORK.
WHAT IS THE WATER PROJECT?
VOLUME
A LOT OF COMMUNITIES IN AFRICA DON'T HAVE ACCESS TO CLEAN WATER. SOMETIMES, PEOPLE HAVE TO WALK HOURS TO A WATER SOURCE AND THEN CARRY IT BACK.
THE WATER PROJECT DOES THINGS LIKE DIG WELLS AND BUILD WATER TANKS. IT MAKES A BIG DIFFERENCE.

LATER THAT EVENING...
HOW CAN I HELP? WHAT CAN I DO? I'M JUST A KID!
I KNOW!
I CAN SELL ALL MY EXTRA SOCCER EQUIPMENT.
AND SOME TOYS!
AND...

THREE DAYS LATER...
To benefit The Water Project
THIS STUFF IS GREAT! WHY ARE YOU SELLING IT?
I'M RAISING MONEY FOR THE WATER PROJECT! I HEARD ABOUT IT FROM THE SUPER FALCONS.
DO YOU THINK YOU CAN REALLY HELP? IT'S NOT LIKE YOU'RE GOING TO GET A LOT OF MONEY.
WHATEVER I GET WILL HELP. WHY DON'T YOU DO IT? IMAGINE HOW MUCH MONEY WE COULD RAISE IF ALL OUR FRIENDS SOLD STUFF THEY DON'T USE OR NEED ANYMORE!
HMM...

Back to Nonfiction

Protectors of Human Rights

The United Nations is a global organization for countries. It created two documents to protect human rights. While the governments of countries can define certain rights for people, such as voting rights, some rights extend to all humans, no matter where they live.

Universal Declaration of Human Rights

The Universal Declaration of Human Rights was adopted in 1948. It lays out basic human rights for all people. First, it says, "All human beings are born free and equal in dignity and rights." It prohibits slavery and cruel punishment. It calls for freedom of religion and opinion. It states that everyone has a right to an education. Other specific rights include freedom from discrimination. All people have a right to be free. They have a right to be safe.

Eleanor Roosevelt holds the Universal Declaration of Human Rights.

The United Nations

The United Nations was created after World War II. The idea was to prevent the kind of war that kills many people and devastates countries. In other words, its basic mission is to maintain peace. All but two countries belong to the UN. That's 193 countries! Its headquarters are in New York City.

Convention on the Rights of the Child

The United Nations Convention on the Rights of the Child was adopted in 1989. A child is a young person through age 17. Children have many of the same rights as adults. But they are not just small adults. The Convention says that childhood is a "special protected time, in which children must be allowed to grow, learn, play, develop and flourish with dignity." All children should be able to grow and thrive. They have a right to an education, and they can have their own opinions. Children have the right to be protected from violence and abuse. They cannot be forced to do dangerous work. And they should have time to play and rest.

Children work in a shipyard in Bangladesh.

Human Rights Watch

Human Rights Watch focuses on defending the rights of people around the world.

In the past, when **refugee** children came to Greece without an adult, they were turned over to the police. They were held in small, overcrowded, dirty cells. Sometimes, they had to share cells with criminals. But these children had a right to be safe. So, an organization called Human Rights Watch got involved. It demanded an end to the practice. It launched a social media campaign. It succeeded. The Greek government changed its practice. Now, children are placed in safe, child-friendly settings.

The work of organizations such as Human Rights Watch needs people with many different skills. Legal experts figure out how laws apply. Experts in society and culture try to understand the history of the situation. **Social workers** help people. Scientists may play a role, too. **Journalists** investigate and write about what's going on. Photographs and videos help tell the story. Social media experts help communicate about events. Office workers keep the organization functioning. Other people raise money to pay for the organization's work. They all care about protecting human rights.

For the Children

UNICEF is an agency of the United Nations. Its focus is on the rights and well-being of children. Its work is to save children's lives, defend their rights, and help them fulfill their potential. When children need help, UNICEF never gives up.

Refugee children attend school in Greece.

Doctors Without Borders

Doctors Without Borders aims to provide global medical care to people in need.

When **measles** broke out in the Democratic Republic of Congo in 2019, it was a true crisis. Measles is one of the most **contagious** diseases in the world. It is especially dangerous for babies, young children, and pregnant women. There is an effective **vaccine** to prevent measles. But access to the vaccine was very limited. Hundreds of thousands of people and children were sick. Thousands had died.

Doctors Without Borders saw the need for help. Teams were sent to the country. This included doctors, nurses, and nonmedical staff, too. During the 2019–2020 **epidemic**, they treated thousands of sick people. They vaccinated more than 2.3 million children. They helped in hospitals. They went to areas where there were no medical facilities or doctors.

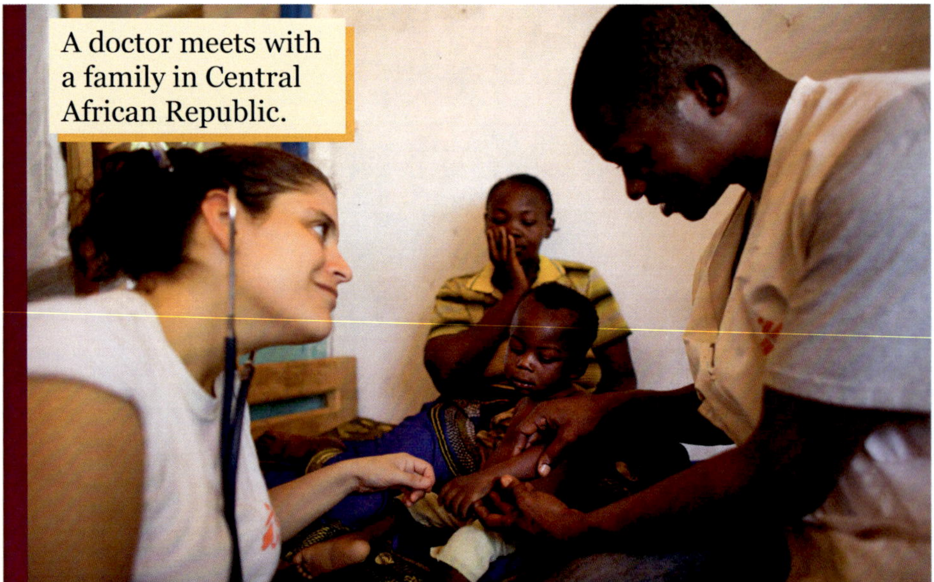

A doctor meets with a family in Central African Republic.

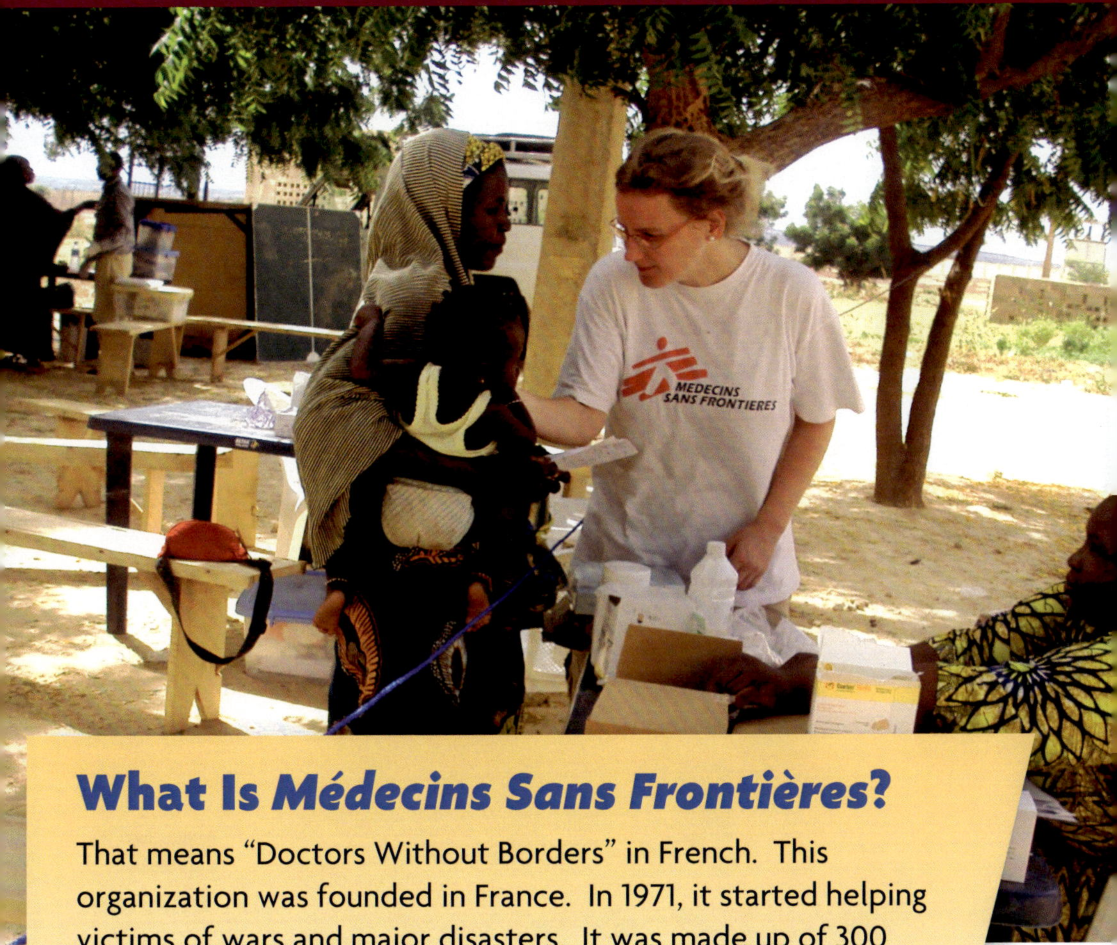

What Is *Médecins Sans Frontières?*

That means "Doctors Without Borders" in French. This organization was founded in France. In 1971, it started helping victims of wars and major disasters. It was made up of 300 volunteers, including doctors, nurses, and staff. Soon after, they opened in more countries.

Medical care is a basic human right. Receiving it can often be an overwhelming challenge. That's why Doctors Without Borders exists. They go places in the world where their help is most needed. The work is always difficult. Often, it is dangerous. They go into active war zones. They go where natural disasters have struck. And they go into refugee camps. They go where they can save lives.

Action Against Hunger

Action Against Hunger develops new methods and ideas for helping people in need of food.

In Central America, one region is known as the Dry Corridor. Parts of Guatemala, Honduras, Nicaragua, and El Salvador are in this region. Here, it has always been challenging to feed a family with only the crops a small farm can produce. Parents would sometimes go without food so their children could eat. Now, life is even harder. One cause is climate change. A six-year drought has ruined crops. COVID-19 has made things difficult, too. People have lost their jobs, and food is more expensive.

All people need enough food to eat so they can stay healthy. Action Against Hunger protects this right. It is a nonprofit group that works to end hunger. It conducted surveys in the Dry Corridor region. It found that more than 85 percent of families face hunger. So, its members stepped in to help. They provided food assistance to more than 50,000 people in rural communities. But Action Against Hunger wants to do more. Its goal is to provide families with food and cash directly. It wants to support the communities, too. It wants to strengthen the health systems and small businesses so people can get jobs.

Greenpeace

Greenpeace works to protect the environment by campaigning and developing solutions.

Greenpeace is an organization that has a deep concern for the environment. Greenpeace has gotten involved with many issues over the years and helped the world's oceans, forests, and climate.

By Land and by Sea

Greenpeace works on land *and* water! The organization has three ships. The ships have been used for many things over the years, including research and campaigns. They help draw attention to environmental issues.

Greenpeace rally

One issue Greenpeace has fought for is protecting the animals in the ocean. In the late 1970s, populations of whales were declining. This was because of commercial whaling. Whales were hunted and killed so they could be sold for their meat and blubber, or fat. Greenpeace took action. They wanted to raise awareness of this issue. So, they created campaigns. Their movement known as "Save the Whales" showed the terrible reality of whaling. They even took boats to places where whaling was happening to stop the whales from getting killed. And they got results! In 1982, the International Whaling Commission voted for a ban on commercial whaling.

By working with other **activists**, Greenpeace has changed minds. It has changed business practices. It has changed what governments do. Greenpeace describes what it does as "peaceful, creative confrontation." They never use violence. They aim to promote peace and non-violence. They want to stop pollution and abuse of Earth's natural resources. They want to protect the planet and all life on it.

Amnesty International

Amnesty International vows to protect and uphold human rights around the world.

In South Africa, a mining company saw an opportunity. It discovered **titanium**, a valuable mineral, on land belonging to a group of **indigenous** people in a community called Xolobeni. The company asked the government for a license to mine the land. No one asked the people who lived there for permission. The native people did not want the mine. It would destroy the land. They would have to move.

Nonhle Mbuthuma was a farmer there. The land had been in her family for generations. She became a leader for the people as they resisted the government's action. She said, "If you take my land, you take my identity." She was threatened for speaking out. The government did nothing to protect her.

Nonhle Mbuthuma

Think and Talk

What are some ways you can speak out against injustices?

You've Got Mail

Amnesty International has a campaign called Write for Rights. People from more than 170 countries and territories participate in it. They write letters to ask that people who have stood up for change be released from jail.

Amnesty International was formed to shine a light on human rights violations like this. It stepped in to help. It supported a lawsuit to require the South African government to consult people before mining on their land. It created a **petition** demanding that the government protect Mbuthuma. It was a long struggle. Finally, a South African court ruled in favor of the indigenous people. It was a victory for human rights.

International Red Cross

The Red Cross is the world's largest humanitarian network.

A massive earthquake occurred deep in the Indian Ocean in 2004. It led to a series of **tsunamis**. These fast-moving walls of water destroyed communities in several countries. In Haiti, people faced many disasters in the 2000s: floods, hurricanes, earthquakes, and disease outbreaks. And in many countries, people face the dangers of war or poverty.

That's where the International Red Cross comes in. With **chapters** in 192 countries, the Red Cross is always nearby. Where there is human suffering, the Red Cross rushes in to help. It finds housing for the people who lose their homes. It provides medical care for the sick and injured. It finds mental health services for people in distress. It supplies clothing and other basic needs. It delivers comfort and hope in the face of despair.

The American Red Cross is connected to the International Red Cross.

Wildfire Relief

In the United States, wildfires have been displacing people in record numbers. The American Red Cross helps people in need. They provide food, shelter, and essential items to people who are forced to evacuate.

The International Red Cross has been helping people for more than 150 years. There are three parts of the Red Cross global network. Each part has the same goal: to provide aid to people, regardless of the situation.

International Committee of the Red Cross headquarters

Education Is a Human Right

"I tell my story not because it is unique, but because it is the story of many girls."—Malala Yousafzai

Malala Yousafzai was born in a village in Pakistan. When she was 11 years old, a group called the **Taliban** took over the village. They had extreme views about society. They banned girls from going to school. Anyone who violated their orders was harshly punished.

Yousafzai's family believed that education is a right for all children, including girls. Yousafzai continued to go to school. She also spoke out in support of education for girls. That got her in trouble with the Taliban. When she was 15, she was on a bus going home from school. A gunman entered the bus. He shot her in the head. Yousafzai almost died.

Yousafzai's family moved to England for safety. She became a vocal **advocate** for education for girls. In 2014, she was the youngest person ever to be awarded the **Nobel Peace Prize**. She was just 17. In her speech, she said, "This award is not just for me. It is for those forgotten children who want education. It is for those frightened children who want peace. It is for those voiceless children who want change."

Think and Talk

What issue(s) would you choose to advocate for and why?

Yousafzai gives a speech during the Nobel Peace Prize ceremony.

Young People Demand a Healthy Environment

A healthy environment is a basic human right. Climate change threatens that. When it comes to raising awareness about climate change, young people are leading the way. Yola Mgogwana is one of them.

Mgogwana lives in Cape Town, South Africa. When she was 11 years old, she began to notice changes in the environment. There was more pollution in the air. That's one cause of climate change. Drought was becoming normal. That is a consequence of climate change.

Mgogwana joined the Earthchild Project to learn all she could about what was happening to the environment. She became an activist. She said, "My age does not mean my views on the world are not valid."

"Little Miss Flint"

In Flint, Michigan, lead got into the town's water supply. Many people got sick. In 2016, 8-year-old Mari Copeny wrote a letter to President Barack Obama. She had been advocating for help and awareness. He visited the town and later provided emergency help. The media referred to her as "Little Miss Flint." Now a teenager, Copeny still raises money and awareness for Flint.

Cape Town climate change protest

She joined climate strikes and marches to bring awareness to the problem of climate change. She said, "I'm marching, singing, and shouting for my right to a livable future." She made a speech in front of 2,000 people. She demanded policies to heal and protect the environment. This kind of conversation can happen in any community. It takes just one person to start it.

Yola Mgogwana marches in a protest.

The Never-Ending Quest

Human beings have human rights. There are no exceptions. Anytime people are deprived of those rights, it is wrong. The quest for equality, freedom, safety, and dignity has gone on throughout history. It will never end.

One person who dedicated their life to this quest was John Lewis. He was a Black man from the southern United States. He fought for justice and equality. Before he died, Lewis said, "I have been in some kind of fight—for freedom, equality, basic human rights—for nearly my entire life." There will always be a need for people willing to take up the fight.

That's why human rights organizations are so important. They help determined people come together and solve problems. These organizations need a lot of help. There are many ways for people like you to help! People can donate money. They can volunteer their time. They can raise awareness of issues. Any small action can help make an impact.

Yola Mgogwana marches in a protest.

Making Good Trouble

John Lewis was known for getting into what he called "good trouble." He faced hate and danger as he demanded equal rights for African Americans. He marched against injustice, even when he knew he would be attacked. He went to jail many times. He fought hard for justice and equality.

Glossary

activists—people who use strong actions to support or oppose an issue

advocate—a person who argues for and/or supports a cause or policy

chapters—branches of an organization

contagious—able to be passed from one person to another

discrimination—unjust behavior based on differences, such as race or gender

drought—a long period of time during which there is very little or no rain

epidemic—a rapidly spreading outbreak of disease

indigenous—living naturally or traditionally in a particular place

journalists—people who collect information about and write news stories for newspapers, magazines, television, or radio

measles—a disease that causes fever and red spots on the skin

Nobel Peace Prize—an award given each year to a person or people who have promoted peace

petition—a written document that people sign to show they want something to happen

refugee—someone who has been forced to leave a country because of war or other dangerous conditions

social workers—people who work for organizations that help people who have problems of various kinds

Taliban—a fundamentalist Islamic militia in Afghanistan

titanium—a very strong and light silvery metal

tsunamis—very high, large ocean waves that are usually caused by underwater earthquakes

vaccine—a substance that is injected to protect against a particular disease

Index

Civics in Action

All people want safe, healthy lives. And everyone has the power to help others. How can you help?

1. Think about basic needs that one person, a particular group of people, or a region of the world is lacking. Examples include clean water, medical care, education, food, clothing, and legal help. You can add others.

2. Brainstorm ways in which you can help people meet those needs. Keep in mind that donating money is one way to help, but there are other ways, too.

3. Meet with family members or friends to make a plan to start your helping project. Write the steps involved.

4. Put your plan into action!